WASHINGTON OBSERVATIONS FOR 1872—APPENDIX II.

REPORT

ON THE

DIFFERENCE OF LONGITUDE

BETWEEN

WASHINGTON

AND

DETROIT, MICHIGAN; CARLIN, NEVADA;

AND

AUSTIN, NEVADA.

BY

J. R. EASTMAN,

PROFESSOR OF MATHEMATICS, UNITED STATES NAVY.

WASHINGTON:
GOVERNMENT PRINTING OFFICE.
1874.

REPORT

ON THE

DIFFERENCE OF LONGITUDE

BETWEEN

WASHINGTON

AND

DETROIT, MICHIGAN; CARLIN, NEVADA;

AND

AUSTIN, NEVADA

BY

J. R. EASTMAN,
PROFESSOR OF MATHEMATICS UNITED STATES NAVY

WASHINGTON:
GOVERNMENT PRINTING OFFICE.
1874.

TABLE OF CONTENTS.

REPORT ON THE DIFFERENCE OF LONGITUDE BETWEEN WASHINGTON AND DETROIT, (MICH.,) CARLIN, (NEV.,) AND AUSTIN, (NEV.)

UNITED STATES NAVAL OBSERVATORY,
Washington, D. C., February 26, 1874.

SIR: I have the honor to submit the following report of special work performed, in compliance with the order of the Superintendent of the Observatory, in 1871.

INTRODUCTION.

This work was undertaken, at the request of Maj. C. B. Comstock and Lieut. G. M. Wheeler, United States Engineers, first, to determine, by the telegraphic exchange of clock-signals, the longitude of the observatory of the Lake Survey at Detroit, Mich., in charge of Major Comstock; and, secondly, to determine, by a similar exchange of clock and chronometer signals, the longitude of several stations in Nevada occupied by Lieutenant Wheeler, in charge of explorations in Nevada, Utah, and Arizona.

The observations and computations at this observatory were made by myself, and those at Detroit by Mr. O. B. Wheeler; the observations at Carlin and Austin were made by Mr. E. P. Austin, and the computations are by Dr. F. Kampf.

EXCHANGE OF SIGNALS.

The plan for exchanging signals proposed by General C. B. Comstock contemplated, first, the transmission of signals from Carlin through Detroit to the chronograph in this observatory until four coincidences were obtained between the Carlin mean-time chronometer and the observatory-clock; then seconds-signals from the observatory clock were to be sent through Detroit to Carlin until four more coincidences were obtained; secondly, the observer at Carlin was to observe six time-stars and register his observations on the observatory-chronograph; and, thirdly, a set of signals, similar to the first, was then to be exchanged between Carlin and the Observatory.

The first and third items of this plan were such as could be easily carried out, but the second I considered almost impossible. I made no objection to it, however, for I barely hoped that a favorable combination of circumstances might enable us to test the relative merits of the clock and the star-signals over this long line.

I was notified that the observers at Carlin and Detroit would be ready to work on May 16; but, though it was clear here and at Carlin, we were not able to exchange signals, on account of a series of storms between Washington and Chicago. On May 19 I sent break-circuit signals from the clock to Carlin, but the Carlin observer reported that the signals were "too long" and he could not use them. Make-circuit signals were then tried, but they did not get through; they were only barely perceptible in the Chicago office.

At the suggestion of the observer at Carlin, break-circuit signals were sent at intervals of ten seconds for one minute; then, after an interval of thirty seconds, another set was forwarded, until three sets were sent.

These signals were sent with the ordinary message-key by breaking the circuit, in coincidence with the beat of the clock, as denoted by the sounder in the local circuit.

After sending these signals, the main circuit was broken, and it was impossible to communicate with Carlin again on that night.

On failing to receive signals from Carlin, communication was established with Detroit, and signals exchanged. The observatory-clock and chronograph were so connected with the main circuit that the clock-beats were recorded on the observatory chronograph and also on the chronograph at Detroit.

Seconds-signals were thus sent from the observatory-clock to the Detroit chronograph in two sets, and two similar sets of signals were received on the observatory-chronograph from the Detroit clock.

Much annoyance and difficulty were experienced during the work, especially in that with Carlin, by the frequent interruptions along the line.

On May 23 the observer at Carlin objected to the seconds-signals from the clock, and signals similar to those sent May 19 were transmitted.

Signals were received on the observatory-chronograph from Carlin in spite of the frequent interruptions along the line. A portion of the signals were sent at intervals of ten seconds and the remainder at intervals of five seconds. They were transmitted with the ordinary message-key by breaking the circuit in coincidence with the beat of a mean-time chronometer.

Two sets of signals were exchanged with Detroit in the same way as on May 19.

On May 24 signals were exchanged with Carlin and with Detroit in the same way as on May 23.

The exchange on May 24 finished the work with Detroit and also with Carlin; for, after waiting in vain until June 1 to get another opportunity to exchange signals on one more night with the observatory, Lieutenant Wheeler reported that he should move to his next station.

On June 16 Mr. E. P. Austin occupied a station at Austin, Nev., and on that night signals were exchanged between that station and this observatory, in the same manner as between Carlin and the observatory, except that the signals from the observatory were sent at intervals of ten seconds by the clock, by switching it into the main line just before each tenth second. The weather prevented further exchange of signals with Austin, Nev.

TELEGRAPHIC CONNECTIONS.

Washington to Detroit.

On May 19 and 24 there were repeaters in the circuit at Philadelphia, Pittsburgh, and Cleveland; miles of wire, 829.

On May 23 repeaters were in the circuit at Philadelphia, Pittsburgh, Cincinnati, and Cleveland; miles of wire, 1,250.

Washington to Carlin.

On May 19 and 24 there were repeaters in the circuit at Philadelphia, Pittsburgh, Cleveland, Detroit, Chicago, Omaha, Cheyenne, and Corinne; miles of wire, 2,943.

On May 24 there were repeaters at Philadelphia, Pittsburgh, Cincinnati, Cleveland, Detroit, Chicago, Omaha, Cheyenne, and Corinne; miles of wire, 3,364.

Washington to Austin.

On June 16 there were repeaters in the circuit at Philadelphia, Pittsburgh, Cincinnati, Cleveland, Detroit, Chicago, Omaha, Cheyenne, Corinne, and Reno; miles of wire, 3,847.

OBSERVATIONS TO DETERMINE THE CLOCK-CORRECTION AT THE UNITED STATES NAVAL OBSERVATORY.

The instrument used in the observations is that known as the "meridian transit," which has been in use at the Observatory for many years, and is now situated in the east wing of the building. A description of this instrument may be found in the Washington Astronomical and Meteorological Observations for 1862.

The transit is now employed under the direction of Prof. M. Yarnall, U. S. N., in observing stars for the "General Catalogue;" and as I made my observations for time after the regular work with the instrument was closed for the night, I used the same observations for collimation which he made for the reduction of his regular work.

The system of transit-threads in this instrument is composed of five groups or sets. When the clamp-end of the axis is east, the set which is first reached by a star in its transit above the pole is known as set A, and the others are known as sets B, C, D, and E. When the instrument is reversed the order of the sets is of course reversed, E being first reached by a star; but, in order to avoid confusion, no mention of reversal of sets is made except in the case of the reduction of broken observations. During the early portion of 1871, the equatorial interval between each thread in the five sets, and the mean of sets B, C, and D, were found to be as below:

Thread.	Interval.	Thread.	Interval.	Thread.	Interval.	Thread.	Interval.	Thread.	Interval.
	s.		s.		s.		s.		s.
A_1	37.897			C_1	3.183	D_1	15.146	E_1	30.003
A_2	35.972			C_2	1.654	D_2	17.589	E_2	32.647
A_3	34.308	B_1	19.216	C_3	0.014	D_3	19.110	E_3	34.153
A_4	32.745	B_2	17.563	C_4	1.639			E_4	35.820
A_5	30.205	B_3	15.069	C_5	3.221			E_5	37.693

The clock used is that known as the "Mural Clock," and is situated in the room with the transit. It is connected with the chronograph in the usual way, and closes the circuit at each second, except at the sixtieth second of each minute, when a small ivory lever, on the axis of the escapement-wheel, raises a very delicate spring, which forms a portion of the circuit, and prevents the closing of the circuit at that instant.

The observations of all but circumpolar stars were recorded in the usual manner by the chronograph, which is described in the annual volume for 1862.

In the reduction of the observations for time, whenever a broken set of observations occurred, each thread was reduced separately, by applying the proper interval from the above table. When the clamp is east, the sign of the reduction is + from A_1 to C_3 inclusive.

INSTRUMENTAL CORRECTIONS.

The corrections to the observed transit of a star were derived from the observed and computed errors c', n', and m'.

The error of collimation is represented by c'; the equatorial value of the distance between the line of collimation and the true meridian at the pole, by n'; and the distance between the line of collimation and the true meridian at the equator, by m'.

The quantities represented by n' and m' are used instead of errors of azimuth and level.

By means of a collimating eye-piece, the error of collimation and level was determined by reversing the instrument over a basin of mercury, and measuring, with the right-ascension micrometer, the distance between the central thread and its image reflected from the mercury.

If we let—

c, n, and m represent the corrections obtained from the observed and computed errors c', n', and m';

2Δ, the distance of the central thread west of its image when the clamp-end of the axis is east;

$2\Delta'$, the distance of the central thread west of its image when the clamp-end of the axis is west;

p, the correction for the excess of the radius of the clamp-pivot, $= 0^s.008$;

r, the equatorial distance of the mean of sets B, C, and D from the middle thread, $= 0^s.014$;

a, the correction for diurnal aberration, $= 0^s.016$;

b, the level-correction;

α, the Nautical Almanac place of the star;

α', the observed place of the star;

δ, the declination of the star;

φ, the latitude of the observing-station;

C', the approximate clock-correction; and

C, the clock-correction determined by the observations of each star,

we have the following formulas, which have been used in reducing the observations for time. n was determined from the observations of circumpolar stars. The quantities Δ and Δ' are given in revolutions of the micrometer-head, each revolution being $= 1^s.5865$:

$$c = \tfrac{1}{2}(\Delta - \Delta') - p - r - a \text{ for clamp east.}$$
$$c = -\tfrac{1}{2}(\Delta - \Delta') + p + r - a \text{ for clamp west.}$$

$$b = -\tfrac{1}{2}(\Delta + \Delta') - p \text{ for clamp east.}$$
$$b = -\tfrac{1}{2}(\Delta + \Delta') + p \text{ for clamp west.}$$

$$n = \frac{\alpha - (\alpha' + C' + c \sec \delta)}{\sec \delta}$$

$$m = -n \tan \varphi + b \sec \varphi$$

$$C = \alpha - (\alpha' + m + n \tan \delta + c \sec \delta)$$

Observed Clock-Corrections at the United States Naval Observatory.

Date.	Number.	Object	Seconds of Transit over Wires I.	II	III.	IV.	V.	VI.	VII.	VIII.	IX.	X.	XI.	Mean.	Instrumental Correction.	Observed Place.	Adopted Right Ascension.	Clock-Correction.
1871.			s.	s.	s	s.	s	s	s.	s.	s.	s.	s.	m. s.	s.	s.	h. m. s	s
May 19	1	ε Bootis . . .	1.5	3.3	6.1	19.6	21.4	23.2	25.0	26.8	40.4	43.1	44.8	39 23.20	+ 0.08	23.28	14 39 22.64	− 0.64
	2	β Bootis . . .	. .	. .	. .	3.3	5.3	7.4	9.5	11.6	. .	. .	. .	57 7.42	+ 0.15	7.57	14 57 6.94	− 0.63
	3	β Libræ . . .	46.6	48.2	50.8	3.1	4.6	6.2	7.8	9.6	21.6	24.0	25.5	10 6.17	− 0.07	6.10	15 10 5.42	− 0.68
	4	μ^1 Bootis . . .	15.0	17.0	19.9	35.4	37.2	39.1	41.3	43.2	58.4	1.6	3.6	19 39.25	+ 0.13	39.38	15 19 38.76	− 0.62
	5	α Cor. Borealis .	. .	. .	. .	32.8	35.5	37.0	49.5	52.4	54.0	56.0	58.1	29 15.70	+ 0.06	15.76	15 29 15.11	− 0.65
	6	α Serpentis . .	37.7	39.3	41.8	53.8	55.3	56.9	58.6	0.2	12.2	14.6	16 2	37 56.96	− 0.02	56.94	15 37 56.29	− 0.65
	7	ε Serpentis . .	. .	. .	. .	21.9	23.5	25.2	26.9	28.5	. .	. .	. .	44 25.20	− 0.03	25.17	15 44 24.60	− 0.57
	8	δ Aquilæ . . .	42.4	43.8	46.2	58.5	59.9	1.5	3.0	4.4	16.6	18.8	20.5	19 1.42	− 0.03	1.39	19 19 0.57	− 0.82
	9	κ Aquilæ . . .	39 3	40.9	43.8	55.4	57.2	58.8	0.5	2.2	13.9	16.5	18.2	29 58.79	− 0.06	58.73	19 29 57.93	− 0.80
	10	γ Aquilæ . . .	49.6	51.5	53.8	6.0	7.5	9.1	11.1	12.8	24.6	27.3	28.5	40 9.25	− 0.01	9.24	19 40 8.46	− 0.78
	11	α Aquilæ . . .	11.6	13.1	15.9	27.7	29.3	30.9	32.5	34.1	46.4	48.9	50.5	44 30.99	− 0.01	30.98	19 44 30.19	− 0.79
	12	β Aquilæ . . .	41.0	42.6	45.0	57.0	58.5	0.1	1.8	3.2	15.4	17.8	19.4	49 0.16	− 0.02	0.14	19 48 59.39	− 0.75
	13	λ Ursæ Minoris.	. .	. .	. .	54.5	17.0	40.0	7.0	31.0	. .	. .	. .	53 42.16	+ 14.87	57.03	19 53 56.20	
23	14	η Herculis . .	. .	. .	. .	. .	. .	. .	6.3	9.7	11.9	14.0	16.5	38 27.51	− 0.13	27.38	16 38 30.23	+ 2.85
	15	κ Ophiuchi . .	13.2	14.6	17.0	29.5	31.1	32.6	34.2	35.8	48.0	50.4	52.1	51 32.59	− 0.16	32.43	16 51 35.20	+ 2.77
	16	d Herculis . .	. .	28.3	31.3	45.6	47.6	49.5	51.5	53.4	7.8	10.8	. .	56 49.55	− 0.13	49.42	16 56 52.28	+ 2.86
	17	a^1 Herculis . .	25.1	26.5	. .	41.3	43.0	44.8	46.5	48.0	0.3	2.8	. .	8 44.74	− 0 15	44.59	17 8 47.40	+ 2.81
	18	δ Ursæ Minoris.	51.0	16.5	58.0	20.5	45.0	14.0	44.0	6.5	29.5	11.0	40.0	14 14.18	− 0.77	13.41	18 14 16.13	
	19	δ Aquilæ . . .	. .	. .	. .	13.2	15.7	17.3	28.5	31.0	32.5	. .	36.1	18 58.17	− 0.16	58.01	19 19 0.68	+ 2.67
	20	γ Aquilæ . . .	46.6	48.1	50.5	2.7	4.5	6.1	7.7	9.2	21.5	23.8	25.6	40 6.03	− 0.15	5.88	19 40 8.57	+ 2.69
	21	α Aquilæ . . .	8.4	9.8	12.2	24.5	26.1	27.7	29.4	31.0	43.0	45.7	47.1	44 27.72	− 0.16	27.56	19 44 30.30	+ 2.74
	22	β Aquilæ . . .	37.8	39.3	41.7	53.9	55.4	57.0	58.6	0.2	12.2	14.6	16.3	48 57.00	− 0.16	56.84	19 48 59.50	+ 2.66
	23	τ Aquilæ . . .	29.3	30.8	33.2	45.4	46.9	48.5	50.1	51.7	3.6	. .	7.8	57 48.51	− 0.16	48.35	19 57 51.13	+ 2.78
24	24	α Serpentis . .	35.1	36.4	39.0	51.1	52.5	54.1	55.8	57.2	9.5	12.1	13.9	37 54.25	− 0.11	54.14	15 37 56.33	+ 2.19
	25	ε Serpentis . .	3.4	4.9	7.4	19.5	21.0	22.7	24.2	25.7	37.8	40.3	42.1	44 22.64	− 0.11	22.53	15 44 24.66	+ 2.13
	26	ε Cor. Borealis .	52.9	54.6	57.2	10.9	12.5	14.4	16.2	18.1	31.5	34.3	36.2	52 14.44	− 0.09	14.35	15 52 16.43	+ 2.08
	27	δ Ophiuchi . .	15.5	17.1	19.7	31.5	33.1	34.7	36.2	37.8	49.8	52.2	54.0	7 34.69	− 0.13	34 56	16 7 36.67	+ 2.11
	28	δ Ursæ Minoris .	. .	. .	. .	21.0	48.5	14.5	40.0	9.0	. .	. .	. .	14 14.66	− 0.51	14.15	18 14 16.26	
	29	α Lyræ . . .	9.3	11.1	14.2	29.6	31.5	33.6	35.8	37.7	53.1	56.1	58.3	32 33.66	− 0.08	33.58	18 32 35.79	+ 2.21
	30	β Lyræ . . .	55.4	57.3	0.3	14.5	16.3	18.4	20.3	22.3	36.4	39.4	41.5	45 18.37	− 0.09	18.28	18 45 20.43	+ 2.15
June 16	31	a^1 Herculis . .	29.7	31.4	34.1	46.3	47 9	49.7	51.4	52.9	5.3	7.8	9.6	8 49.64	+ 0.22	49.86	17 8 47.65	− 2.21
	32	α Ophiuchi . .	40.6	42.7	45.2	57.3	58.9	0.5	2.3	4.0	16.0	18.6	20.2	29 0.57	+ 0.21	0.78	17 28 58.52	− 2.26
	33	μ Herculis . .	. .	. .	. .	25.0	26.5	28.2	30.1	32.0	45.5	48.2	50.0	41 28.35	+ 0.30	28.65	17 41 26.42	− 2.23
	34	δ Ursæ Minoris .	. .	. .	. .	21.5	48.0	15.0	41.5	9.0	. .	. .	. .	14 15.00	+ 4.92	19.92	18 14 17.67	
	35	ι Aquilæ . . .	. .	. .	. .	11.8	13.3	15.1	16.7	18.4	30.2	32.9	34.3	28 15.04	+ 0.12	15.16	18 28 12.95	− 2.21
	36	α Lyræ . . .	13.5	15.5	18.9	34.2	36.1	38.0	40.1	42.1	57.3	0.7	2.7	32 38.10	+ 0.36	38 46	18 32 36.20	− 2.26
	37	β Lyræ . . .	59.7	2.0	4.9	19.1	20.9	22.9	24.9	26.6	41.0	43.9	45.6	45 22.86	+ 0.33	23.19	18 45 20.87	− 2.32
	38	ζ Cygni . . .	7.9	9.8	12.7	26.6	23.2	30.1	32 2	33.8	47.5	50.2	52.0	7 30.09	+ 0.31	30.40	21 7 28.08	− 2.32
	39	ι Pegasi . . .	50.0	51.8	54.4	7.1	8.7	10.5	12.2	14.0	26.6	29.2	31.1	16 10.51	+ 0.24	10.75	21 16 8.45	− 2.30
	40	β Aquarii. . .	29.9	31.5	34.0	46.0	47.6	49.2	50.9	52.5	4.5	7.1	8.5	24 49.25	+ 0.13	49.38	21 24 47.15	− 2.23
	41	ξ Aquarii. . .	36.9	38.5	40.9	53.3	54.7	56.2	57.8	59.5	. .	. .	. .	30 56.27	+ 0.12	56.39	21 30 54.09	− 2 30
	42	ε Pegasi . . .	34.8	35.5	38.9	51.0	52.6	54 2	55.8	57.4	9.5	11.8	13.5	37 54.17	+ 0.20	54.37	21 37 52.09	− 2.28

REMARKS.

Nos. 2, 7, 13, 23, set C.
14, set E.
16, B_1 and D_1 rejected.
17, B_3 and D_3 rejected.
19, sets D and E, E_1 rejected.
23, D_1 rejected.
33, sets C and D.
34, set C. Cloudy.
35, sets C and D.
41, sets B and C.
On May 23 and 24 the stars were very unsteady.

COLLIMATION.

May 19.9 Image east $0^r.16$, clamp east.
May 19.9. Image west $0^r.19$, clamp west.
May 23.9. Image west $0^r.17$, clamp west.
May 24.9. Image west $0^r.19$, clamp west.
May 24.9. Image east $0^r.10$, clamp east.
June 16.9. Image west $0^r.20$, clamp east.
June 16.9. Image west $0^r.42$, clamp west.
On May 19 and June 16 the clamp was east, and on May 23 and 24 it was west.

The values of m, n, and c, used in the reductions, are as follows:

Date.		m	n	c
		s.	s.	s.
May	19	− 0.143	+ 0.184	+ 0.102
	23	− 0.046	+ 0.088	− 0.114
	24	− 0.010	+ 0.082	− 0.110
June	16	+ 0.113	+ 0.242	+ 0.050

From the clock-corrections obtained from the observations the following clock-corrections and hourly rates were computed by the method of least squares. These corrections and rates have been employed to determine the error of the clock at the time of the interchange of signals on each night:

Date.		Sidereal Hour.	Correction.	Hourly Rate.
		h.	s. s.	s.
May	19	14.0	− 0.594 ± 0.007	− 0.034
	23	16.0	+ 2.854 ± 0.010	− 0.039
	24	15.0	+ 2.117 ± 0.012	+ 0.016
June	16	17.0	− 2.234 ± 0.007	− 0.012

LONGITUDE OF DETROIT, MICHIGAN.

Clock-Corrections and Rates at Detroit.

The following extract from a letter from Major Comstock gives the location of the observatory at Detroit; a description of the instruments; a list of stars observed, together with the method of reduction; the observed places of the clock-stars; and the deduced clock corrections and rates:

The instrument used here in determining the clock-correction was a portable transit of the Troughton & Simms make; the focal length of its object-glass being 42 inches. The sidereal clock and the chronograph were, respectively, Nos. 184 and 216, Bond & Son. The length of the cylinder of the chronograph is 13.8 inches, its diameter 6 inches, and it records for two and one-half hours without change of paper.

The present Lake-Survey observatory is situated on Grand River avenue, in rear of the Lake-Survey office, and was built in March of the present year. The east-transit stone pier used in this connection is 143.7 feet (equal to $0^s.127$) west, and 146.6 feet (equal to $1''.45$) north of the west-transit pier of the former observatory, and 321.0 feet (equal to $0^s.285$) west, and 294.0 feet (equal to $2''.906$) north from the southwest corner of the stone foundation of the Westminster Church, on Washington avenue. The observatory is near a paved street, on which loaded wagons and street-cars are passing until a late hour. On this account, stars observed before Polaris were rejected; there being two on the 19th, one on the 23d, and one on the 24th.

Owing to the disturbances incident to the situation of the observatory, the daily rate of the clock has been considered of no value from the beginning. The rate, however, during the time of observation on any night when the disturbances had nearly ceased, may be considered as uniform.

The clock-corrections and the instrumental errors were deduced by the method of least squares; the rate of the clock being retained as an unknown quantity.

In the following tables—

$C\Delta i$ = reduction to middle wire;
Aberr. = diurnal aberration;
$(t_1 - t_2)\rho$ = correction for rate to mean of observed times;
$A\,a$ = correction for azimuth;
$B\,b$ = correction for level;
$C\,c$ = correction for collimation;
t' = observed time, or mean of five wires;
α = right ascension;
Δt = clock-correction; and
v = residuals obtained from mean Δt.

Computation of Clock-Correction for Clock No. 184, *May* 19, 1871.

Ill.	Star.	$C\Delta i$	Aberr.	$(t_1-t_2)\rho$	$A\,a$	$B\,b$	$C\,c$	t'	α	Δt	v
		s.	s.	s.	s.	s.	s.	h. m. s.	s.	s.	s.
E.	Polaris, L. C. . .	. .	+0.58	+0.43	+2.88	+2.01	+0.29	13 11 24.75	59.40	−31.54	0.00
W.	Polaris, L. C. . .	. .	+0.58	+0.40	+2.88	−2.23	−0.29	11 29.60	. .	−31.54	0.00
	ζ Virginis . . .	+0.03	−0.01	+0.37	+0.06	+0.06	+0.01	28 39.41	8.37	−31.56	+0.02
	η Ursæ Majoris .	+0.05	−0.02	+0.33	−0.02	+0.15	+0.01	42 59.87	29.05	−31.32	−0.22
	η Bootis. . . .	+0.03	−0.02	+0.32	+0.04	+0.13	+0.01	49 4.80	33.80	−31.51	−0.03
	τ Virginis . . .	+0.03	−0.01	+0.30	+0.06	+0.12	+0.01	13 55 37.29	6.13	−31.67	+0.13
	ρ Bootis. . . .	+0.04	−0.02	+0.22	+0.03	+0.25	+0.01	14 26 48.85	17.67	−31.71	+0.17
W.	ε Bootis. . . .	+0.03	−0.02	+0.19	+0.03	+0.20	+0.01	39 53.85	22.66	−31.63	+0.09
E.	β Bootis. . . .	−0.04	−0.02	+0.15	0.00	+0.09	−0.01	14 57 38.34	6.91	−31.60	+0.06
	β Libræ	−0.03	−0.01	+0.12	+0.07	+0.05	−0.01	15 10 36.60	5.42	−31.37	−0.17
	μ^1 Bootis. . . .	−0.04	−0.02	+0.10	+0.01	+0.09	−0.01	20 10.24	38.76	−31.61	+0.07
	α Serpentis . . .	−0.03	−0.02	+0.05	+0.05	+0.07	−0.01	38 27.62	56.27	−31.46	−0.08
	ε Serpentis . . .	−0.03	−0.01	+0.03	+0.05	+0.07	−0.01	15 44 55.94	24.62	−31.42	−0.12
	δ Ophiuchi . . .	−0.03	−0.01	−0.03	+0.06	+0.07	−0.01	16 8 7.94	36.60	−31.39	−0.15
	ζ Aquilæ . . .	−0.03	−0.01	−0.45	+0.05	+0.14	−0.01	19 0 1.73	29.82	−31.60	+0.06
	ω Aquilæ . . .	−0.03	−0.01	−0.48	+0.05	+0.11	−0.01	12 18 40	46.62	−31.41	−0.13
	γ Aquilæ . . .	−0.03	−0.01	−0.55	+0.05	+0.16	−0.01	40 40.43	8.43	−31.61	+0.07
	α Aquilæ . . .	−0.03	−0.01	−0.57	+0.05	+0.15	−0.01	45 2.14	30.15	−31.57	+0.03
E.	β Aquilæ . . .	−0.03	−0.01	−0.58	+0.05	+0.15	−0.01	19 49 31.56	59.36	−31.77	+0.23
										−31.54	

$a = +\ 0^s.092$ = Azimuth constant.
$c = -\ 0^s.007$ = Collimation constant.
$\rho = +\ 0^s.1493$ = Rate per hour.
$\Delta t = -\ 31^s.540$ Reduced to $15^h\ 57^m$.
$p = 15.685$ = Weight of Δt.
$r = \pm\ 0^s.023$ = Probable error of Δt.

Computation of Clock-Correction for Clock No. 184, *May* 23, 1871.

Ill.	Star.	C△i	Aberr.	$(t_1-t_2)\rho$	A a	B b	C c	t'	a	△t	v
		s.	s.	s.	s.	s.	s.	h. m. s.	s.	s.	s.
E.	Polaris, L. C. . .	. .	+0.58	+0.44	−11.92	−1.56	+0.83	13 11 55.87	2.14	−42.10	+0.02
W.	Polaris, L. C. . .	. .	+0.58	+0.41	−11.92	−3.78	−0.83	11 59.76	. .	−42.08	0.00
	ζ Virginis . . .	+0.03	−0.01	+0.38	− 0.26	+0.12	+0.02	28 50.01	8.36	−41.93	−0.15
	η Ursæ Minoris .	+0.05	−0.02	+0.35	+ 0.08	+0.30	+0.03	43 10.32	29.00	−42.11	+0.03
	η Bootis. . . .	+0.03	−0.01	+0.33	− 0.16	+0.19	+0.02	49 15.43	33.79	−42.04	−0.04
	τ Virginis . . .	+0.03	−0.01	+0.31	− 0.24	+0.17	+0.02	13 55 47.91	6.13	−42.06	−0.02
W.	α Bootis. . . .	+0.03	−0.01	+0.27	− 0.16	+0.26	+0.02	14 10 29.69	47.92	−42.18	+0.10
E.	5 Ursæ Minoris .	−0.13	−0.06	+0.23	+ 0.90	+0.52	−0.08	28 35.24	54.47	−42.15	+0.07
	α² Libræ	−0.03	−0.01	+0.20	− 0.34	+0.08	−0.02	44 28.17	46.09	−41.96	−0.12
	ψ Bootis. . . .	−0.04	−0.02	+0.16	− 0.11	+0.16	−0.02	14 59 38.71	56.60	−42.24	+0.16
	β Libræ	−0.03	−0.01	+0.13	− 0.30	+0.08	−0.02	15 10 47.54	5.45	−41.94	−0.14
	μ¹ Bootis. . . .	−0.04	−0.02	+0.11	− 0.04	+0.14	−0.03	20 20.95	38.77	−42.30	+0.22
	α Coronæ Borealis.	−0.04	−0.02	+0.08	− 0.11	+0.11	−0.02	29 57.40	15.13	−42.27	+0.19
	α Serpentis . . .	−0.03	−0.01	+0.06	− 0.22	+0.07	−0.02	38 38.46	56.30	−42.01	−0.07
	ε Serpentis . . .	−0.03	−0.01	+0.05	− 0.24	+0.07	−0.02	45 6.77	24.65	−41.94	−0.14
	ε Coronæ Borealis.	−0.04	−0.02	+0.03	− 0.11	+0.10	−0.02	15 52 58.65	16.49	−42.10	+0.02
	d Sagittarii . . .	−0.03	−0.02	−0.45	− 0.35	+0.11	−0.02	19 10 49.10	6.29	−42.05	−0.03
	ω Aquilæ . . .	−0.03	−0.01	−0.46	− 0.20	+0.18	−0.02	12 29.52	46.73	−42.25	+0.17
E.	δ Aquilæ . . .	−0.03	−0.01	−0.48	− 0.24	+0.16	−0.02	19 43.29	0.63	−42.04	−0.04
W.	κ Aquilæ . . .	+0.03	−0.01	−0.51	− 0.30	+0.13	+0.02	30 40.48	58.00	−41.84	−0.24
	γ Aquilæ . . .	+0.03	−0.01	−0.53	− 0.21	+0.17	+0.02	40 51.03	8.54	−41.96	−0.12
	α Aquilæ . . .	+0.03	−0.01	−0.54	− 0.22	+0.19	+0.02	45 12.87	30.26	−42.08	0.00
W.	β Aquilæ . . .	+0.03	−0.01	−0.55	− 0.23	+0.20	+0.02	19 49 42.12	59.47	−42.11	+0.03
										−42.08	

$a = -$ 0ˢ.381 = Azimuth constant.
$c = -$ 0ˢ.020 = Collimation constant.
$\rho = +$ 0ˢ.1471 = Rate per hour.
$\triangle t = -$ 42ˢ.080 Reduced for rate to 16ʰ 4ᵐ.
$p =$ 20.161 = Weight of $\triangle t$.
$r = \pm$ 0ˢ.019 = Probable error of $\triangle t$.

Computation of Clock-Correction for Clock No. 184, May 24, 1871.

Ill.	Star.	C△i	Aberr.	$(t_1-t_2)\rho$	A a	B b	C c	t'	a	△t	v
		s.	s.	s.	s.	s.	s.	h. m. s.	s.	s.	s.
W.	Polaris, L. C. . .	. .	+0.58	+0.27	−8.20	−3.78	−2.69	13 12 1.85	2.74	−45.29	+0.01
E.	Polaris, L. C. . .	. .	+0.58	+0.25	−8.20	−2.23	+2.69	11 54.94	. .	−45.29	+0.01
	ζ Virginis . . .	−0.03	−0.01	+0.24	−0.18	+0.09	−0.07	28 53.43	8.35	−45.12	−0.16
	η Bootis. . . .	−0.03	−0.02	+0.20	−0.11	+0.12	−0.07	13 49 18.88	33.78	−45.19	−0.09
	α Bootis. . . .	−0.03	−0.02	+0.17	−0.11	+0.12	−0.07	14 10 33.12	47.92	−45.26	−0.02
	ρ Bootis. . . .	−0.04	−0.02	+0.14	−0.06	+0.14	−0.07	27 3.00	17.66	−45.43	+0.15
	ε Bootis. . . .	−0.04	−0.02	+0.12	−0.08	+0.14	−0.07	40 7.97	22.66	−45.36	+0.08
E.	α² Libræ	−0.03	−0.01	+0.11	−0.23	+0.07	−0.07	44 31.33	46.09	−45.08	−0.20
W.	β Bootis. . . .	+0.04	−0.02	+0.09	−0.01	+0.22	+0.09	14 57 51.88	6.90	−45.39	+0.11
	β Libræ	+0.03	−0.01	+0.07	−0.21	+0.13	+0.07	15 10 50.52	5.45	−45.15	−0.13
	μ¹ Bootis. . . .	+0.04	−0.02	+0.06	−0.03	+0.31	+0.08	20 23.66	38.78	−45.32	+0.04
	α Coronæ Borealis.	+0.04	−0.02	+0.04	−0.08	+0.31	+0.07	30 0.16	15.14	−45.38	+0.10
	α Serpentis . . .	+0.03	−0.01	+0.02	−0.15	+0.23	+0.07	38 41.54	56.31	−45.42	+0.14
	ε Coronæ Borealis.	+0.04	−0.02	0.00	−0.08	+0.31	+0.07	53 1.54	16.49	−45.37	+0.09
	β Scorpii . . .	+0.03	−0.02	−0.01	−0.25	+0.14	+0.07	15 58 43.04	57.84	−45.16	−0.12
	δ Ophiuchi . . .	+0.03	−0.01	−0.02	−0.19	+0.20	+0.07	16 8 21.86	36.65	−45.29	+0.01
	d Sagittarii . . .	+0.03	−0.02	−0.32	−0.24	+0.07	+0.07	19 10 51.83	6.32	−45.10	−0.18
W.	ω Aquilæ . . .	+0.03	−0.01	−0.33	−0.14	+0.10	+0.07	12 32.20	46.75	−45.17	−0.11
E.	γ Aquilæ . . .	−0.03	−0.01	−0.37	−0.14	+0.08	−0.07	40 54.43	8.57	−45.32	+0.04
	α Aquilæ . . .	−0.03	−0.01	−0.38	−0.15	+0.08	−0.07	45 16.21	30.29	−45.36	+0.08
E.	β Aquilæ . . .	−0.03	−0.01	−0.39	−0.16	+0.07	−0.07	19 49 45.57	59.50	−45.48	+0.20
										−45.28	

$a = -$ 0ˢ.262 = Azimuth constant.
$c = -$ 0ˢ.065 = Collimation constant.
$\rho = +$ 0ˢ.0983 = Rate per hour.
$\Delta t = -$ 45ˢ.280 Reduced for rate to 15ʰ 54ᵐ.
$p =$ 17ˢ.922 = Weight of Δt.
$r = \pm$ 0ˢ.020 = Probable error of Δt.

On the 23d there was one star rejected, and six on the 24th, five of which were zenith-stars; and the tortuous position in observing these stars gives a sufficient excuse for rejecting them. A former reduction, also by least squares, where all the stars were retained, made the final longitude greater by only 0ˢ.02.

The following table presents the clock corrections and rates, as furnished by Major Comstock:

Date.		By Clock.	Clock-Correction.	Rate per Hour.
		h. m.	s. s.	s.
May	19	15 57	− 31.54 ± 0.023	+ 0.1493
	23	16 4	− 42.08 ± 0.019	+ 0.1471
	24	15 54	− 45.28 ± 0.020	+ 0.0983

The data in the above table have been used in computing the Detroit clock-corrections in the following comparison of signals.

The time given in these comparisons for each clock is the mean of eleven signals, read from the chronograph-sheets.

In August, 1871, Mr. O. B. Wheeler and I observed on three nights, at this observatory, for the purpose of finding the value of our personal equation, but the results were not so accordant as would warrant their use in this work. It was evident, however, that the true personal equation was very small.

Date.	Signals sent from—	Time of Mean of Signals by Washington Clock.	Correction of Washington Clock.	Local Sidereal Time of Mean of Signals.	Time of Mean of Signals by Detroit Clock.	Correction of Detroit Clock.	Local Sidereal Time of Mean of Signals.	Differences of Longitude.	Wave and Armature Time.	Final Difference of Longitude.
1871.		h. m. s.	s.	h. m. s.	h. m. s.	s.	h. m. s.	m. s.	s.	m. s.
May 19	W. to D.	18 49 59.03	− 0.76	18 49 58.27	18 26 30.00	− 31.91	18 25 58.09	24 0.18	0.16	24 0.34
	D. to W.	19 0 59.32	− 0.76	19 0 58.56	18 37 30.00	− 31.94	18 36 58.06	24 0.50		
23	W. to D.	18 58 38.85	+ 2.74	18 58 41.59	18 35 24.00	− 42.45	18 34 41.55	24 0.04	0.13	24 0.17
	D. to W.	19 4 45.10	+ 2.73	19 4 47.83	18 41 30.00	− 42.47	18 40 47.53	24 0.30		
24	W. to D.	18 1 12.30	+ 2.17	18 1 14.47	17 38 0.00	− 45.45	17 37 14.55	23 59.92	0.16	24 0.08
	D. to W.	18 15 12.60	+ 2.17	18 15 14.77	17 52 0.00	− 45.47	17 51 14.53	24 0.24		
								Mean	0.15	24 0.20

The Washington transit-instrument is 42.7 feet east of the center of the dome of the observatory; and that distance, in this latitude, is equal to $0^s.036$. Therefore, the transit-instrument in the Lake-Survey observatory in Detroit is west of the center of the dome of the Naval Observatory—

$$0^h\ 24^m\ 0^s.16$$

LONGITUDE OF CARLIN AND OF AUSTIN, NEVADA.

The latitude, description of instruments, methods of reducing the observations, and the computations of the corrections and rates of chronometers at Carlin and Austin, are simply copied, save in a very few instances, from the data and computations furnished by Lieut. G. M. Wheeler.

CARLIN, NEVADA.

Latitude, $+ 40° \ 42' \ 26''.7$.

This station is situated on the bank of a small creek about 250 feet north of the railroad-track and 2,500 feet from the Humboldt River. The valley here is rather wide and comparatively level. The nearest hill of any consequence lies in the southwest.

The instrument used was a combined transit, made by Würdemann, of 26.0 inches focal length and 1.75 inches aperture, and bearing the number 16. It was mounted on four pieces of redwood scantling, 4 by 4 inches, which were set in the ground about four feet and fastened above by cross-pieces of board.

Observations for time were made by means of a sidereal chronometer, Negus No. 1344. For exchange of signals a mean solar chronometer, Hutton No. 288, was always used.

The weather was cloudy most of the time. The clear nights were very cold, and often windy.

The observations were conducted in a common wall-tent. The telegraphic apparatus and the chronometers were kept in the same tent.

Owing to the great range of temperature during the day, being often inside the tent 80° to 90°, the rates of the chronometers were very unsteady.

In the following tables, showing the observations and the deduced chronometer-corrections at Carlin and Austin—

T = the observed time, reduced to the mean of the wires and corrected for rate;
b B = correction for level of the instrument;
a A = correction for azimuth of the instrument;
c C = correction for collimation of the instrument;
T′ = corrected time of star-observations;
α = right ascension of the star; and
ΔT = resulting correction of chronometer.

CARLIN, *May* 19, 1871.

Name of Star.	Clamp.	T	*b* B	*a* A	*c* C	T′	*α*	ΔT
		h. m. s.	s.	s.	s.	h. m. s.	h. m. s.	m. s.
o Virginis. . .	E.	11 53 46.09	+0.06	+ 9.70	−0.23	11 53 55.62	11 58 38.97	+ 4 43.35
ε Corvi . . .	.	11 58 29.58	+0.02	+ 17.65	−0.25	11 58 47.00	12 3 30.55	43.55
4 Draconis . .	.	12 2 24.58	+0.12	− 55.78	−1.14	12 1 27.78	6 10.99	43.21
13 Comæ . . .	.	13 3.16	0.00	+ 4.95	−0.26	13 7.85	17 50.99	43.14
δ Corvi. . . .	.	18 13.30	−0.04	+ 15.99	−0.24	18 29.01	23 12.86	43.85
β Corvi. . . .	.	22 36.70	−0.07	+ 17.87	−0.25	22 54.25	27 37.80	43.55
21 Cassiopeæ, L. C.	W.	31 24.60	−0.20	+ 61.85	−0.85	32 25.20	37 7.33	42.13
32 Camelopardalis.	.	45 37.38	+0.56	−122.48	+2.22	43 37.68	12 48 20.57	42.89
θ Virginis . . .	.	12 58 20.47	+0.02	+ 13.21	+0.23	12 58 33.93	13 3 17.38	43.45
α Virginis . . .	.	13 13 26.94	+0.04	+ 14.61	+0.23	13 13 41.82	13 18 25.07	43.25
ζ Virginis . . .	.	13 23 12.64	+0.07	+ 12.01	+0.23	13 23 24.95	13 28 8.37	+ 4 43.42

For $12^h\ 40^m$ local sidereal time the mean correction is $= +\ 4^m\ 43^s.254$.

Excluding the circumpolar stars, the correction is $= +\ 4^m\ 43^s.445$.

Normal Equations.

$$0 = -\ 2.51 + 11.00\,\delta t - 0.57\,a' + 1.28\,c$$
$$0 = +\ 18.44 - 0.57\,\delta t + 68.94\,a' + 62.19\,c$$
$$0 = +\ 35.55 + 1.28\,\delta t + 62.19\,a' + 140.36\,c$$

Whence—

$$\delta t = +\ 0^s.254$$
$$a' = -\ 0^s.058$$
$$c = -\ 0^s.230$$

The assumed azimuth constant was $+\ 18^s.50$; consequently, the adopted azimuth constant was $+\ 18^s.442$.

CARLIN, *May* 23, 1871.

Name of Star.	Clamp.	T	bB	aA	cC	T′	a	ΔT
		h. m. s.	s.	s.	s.	h. m. s.	h. m. s.	m. s.
Ophiuchi	E.	16 25 20.82	− 0.02	+ 4.66	− 0.01	16 25 25.25	16 30 4.89	+ 4 39.64
Herculis	W.	33 49.96	− 0.22	+ 0.20	+ 0.02	33 49.96	38 30.22	40.26
Ophiuchi	.	43 12.84	− 0.17	+ 2.90	+ 0.01	43 15.58	47 55.84	40.26
Ophiuchi	.	46 52.46	− 0.18	+ 2.96	+ 0.01	46 55.25	51 35.16	39.91
Ursæ Minoris . .	.	16 55 14.38	− 0.72	−27.78	+ 0.08	16 54 45.96	16 59 25.94	39.98
Herculis	.	17 4 4.77	− 0.15	+ 2.58	+ 0.01	17 4 7.21	17 8 47.38	40.17
Draconis	E.	17 33 13.82	− 0.63	− 7.35	− 0.03	17 33 5.81	17 37 46.01	+ 4 40.20

For $17^h\ 0^m$ local sidereal time the mean correction is $+ 4^m\ 40^s.060$.

Normal Equations.

$$0 = -\ 1.90 + 7.00\,\delta t - 3.90\,a' - 7.97\,c$$
$$0 = +\ 10.25 - 3.90\,\delta t + 27.26\,a' + 32.16\,c$$
$$0 = +\ 12.66 - 7.97\,\delta t + 32.16\,a' + 68.53\,c$$

Whence—

$$\delta t = +\ 0^s.060$$
$$a' = -\ 0^s.353$$
$$c = -\ 0^s.012$$

The assumed azimuth constant was $+ 6^s.00$, and the adopted azimuth constant was therefore $+ 5^s.647$.

CARLIN, *May* 24, 1871.

Name of Star.	Clamp.	T	bB	aA	cC	T′	a	ΔT
		h. m. s.	s.	s.	s.	h. m. s.	h. m. s.	m. s.
Cephi, L. C. . . .	E.	11 29 21.72	+ 1.22	− 4.18	+ 1.32	11 29 20.08	11 34 2.59	+ 4 42.51
Leonis	.	37 49.86	− 0.55	− 0.48	− 0.31	37 48.52	43 29.27	40.75
Ursæ Majoris . .	. .	42 23.65	− 0.97	+ 0.44	− 0.52	42 22.60	47 3.00	40.40
Virginis	.	11 53 59.94	− 0.48	− 0.57	− 0.30	11 53 58.59	11 58 38.92	40.33
Draconis	.	12 1 30.32	− 1.84	+ 3.23	− 1.48	12 1 30.23	12 6 10.58	40.35
Corvi	.	22 58.86	− 0.24	− 1.04	− 0.32	22 57.26	27 37.76	40.50
1 Cassiopeæ, L.C. .	W.	32 31.19	+ 0.34	− 3.57	− 1.11	32 26.85	37 6.05	39.20
2 Camelopardalis . .	.	43 30.87	− 2.68	+ 7.10	+ 2.90	43 38.19	12 48 19.81	41.62
Virginis	.	12 58 37.92	− 0.24	− 0.77	+ 0.30	12 58 37.21	13 3 17.36	40.15
Virginis	.	13 13 45.64	− 0.15	− 0.85	+ 0.31	13 13 44.95	13 18 25.05	+ 4 40.10

For $13^h\ 0^m$ local sidereal time, excluding the circumpolar stars, the mean correction is $+ 4^m\ 40^s.372$.

Normal Equations.

$$0 = +\ 4.22 + 10.00\,\delta t + 0.63\,a$$
$$0 = -\ 89.14 + 0.63\,\delta t + 82.97\,a$$

Whence— $a = -\ 1^s.072$

The adopted error of collimation was $- 0^s.30$.

CARLIN, *May* 24, 1871.

Name of Star.	Clamp.	T	*b*B	*a*A	*c*C	T′	*a*	△T
		h. m. s.	s.	s.	s.	h. m. s.	h. m. s.	m. s.
ε Serpentis	W.	15 40 45.54	− 0.06	− 1.25	+ 0.30	15 40 44.53	15 44 24.65	+ 4 40.12
ζ Ursæ Minoris . .	.	44 1.60	− 0.19	+ 6.32	+ 1.47	44 9.21	48 49.34	40.13
β¹ Scorpii	.	15 53 19.06	− 0.01	− 1.95	+ 0.32	15 53 17.42	15 57 57.84	40.42
δ Ophiuchi	.	16 2 57.60	0.00	− 1.48	+ 0.30	16 2 56.42	16 7 36.65	40.23
τ Herculis	E.	11 14.00	− 0.17	+ 0.32	− 0.44	11 13.71	15 53.70	39.99
η Draconis	.	17 36.72	− 0.24	+ 1.61	− 0.64	17 37.45	22 17.79	40.34
ζ Ophiuchi . . . 7	.	25 26.92	− 0.07	− 1.67	− 0.30	25 24.88	30 4.89	40.01
η Herculis	.	16 33 51.10	− 0.13	− 0.07	− 0.39	16 33 50.51	16 38 30.22	+ 4 39 71

For $16^h\ 10^m$ local sidereal time, the mean correction is $+ 4^m\ 40^s.120$.

Normal Equations.

$$0 = - \ 2.78 + 8.00\,\delta t - \ 0.86\,a$$
$$0 = + 24.99 - 0.86\,\delta t + 11.74\,a$$

Whence—

$$\delta t = + 0^s.120$$
$$a = - 2^s.120$$

The adopted error of collimation was $- 0^s.30$.

The following table contains the adopted corrections and rates of the sidereal chronometer, Negus No. 1344 :

Date.	Local Sidereal Time.	Correction of Chronometer.	Hourly Rate.
1871.	h.	m. s.	s.
May 19	12.667	+ 4 43.445	− 0.034
23	17.000	+ 4 40.060	+ 0.009
24	14.508	+ 4 40.246	+ 0.009

In exchanging signals, mean solar-time chronometer Hutton No. 288 was used. Its corrections and rates were determined by the following comparisons, and are shown in the table:

Date.	Negus No. 1344.	Hutton 288.
	h. m. s.	h. m. s.
May 19, a. m.	0 32 12.0	20 25 21.5
19, p. m.	13 30 20.0	9 21 20.0
19, p. m.	13 33 27.0	9 24 26.5
20, a. m.	1 41 31.0	21 30 29.5
20, a. m.	1 44 34.0	21 33 32.0
May 23, p. m.	13 27 18.0	9 2 24.5
23, p. m.	13 30 25.0	9 5 31.0
23, p. m.	13 33 34.0	9 8 39.5
23, p. m.	16 12 10.0	11 46 49.5
23, p. m.	16 15 15.0	11 49 54.0
May 24, p. m.	13 34 32.0	9 5 37.5
24, p. m.	13 37 35.0	9 8 40.0
2 , p. m.	15 30 19.0	11 1 5.5
24, p. m.	15 33 20.0	11 4 6.0

From these comparisons, and the adopted corrections and rates of Negus No. 1344, the following table is derived:

Date.		Time by Hutton 288.	Hutton 288 *slow* of local Sidereal Time.	Hutton 288 losing per hour.
1871.		h. m. s.	h. m. s.	s.
May	19	9 22 53.25	4 13 43.666	9.9713
	23	10 26 56.72	4 29 47.454	9.8478
	24	10 4 52.25	4 33 44.496	9.8832

These values were used in the following computation of the difference of longitude from the exchange of signals:

Date.	Signals sent from—	Time of Mean of Signals by Washington Clock.	Correction of Washington Clock.	Local Sidereal Time of Mean of Signals.	Time of Mean of Signals by Carlin Chronometer.	Correction of Carlin Chronometer.	Local Sidereal Time of Mean of Signals.	Differences of Longitude.	Means.	Wave and Armature Time.	Final differ'nce of Longitude.
1871.		h. m. s.	s.	h. m. s.	h. m. s.	h. m. s.	h. m. s.	h. m. s.	s.	s.	h. m. s.
May 19	W. to C.	17 36 39.47	− 0.72	17 36 38.75	10 46 24.63	+ 4 13 57.55	15 0 22.18	2 36 16.57			
23	W. to C.	17 40 56.47	+ 2.79	17 40 59.26	10 34 53.81	+ 4 29 48.76	15 4 42.57	2 36 16.69			
		18 37 30.00	+ 2.75	18 37 32.75	11 31 18.02	+ 4 29 58.02	16 1 16.04	2 36 16.71	16.70		
										0.62	2 36 17.32
	C. to W.	17 55 44.24	+ 2.78	17 55 47.02	10 49.37.97	+ 4 29 51.18	15 19 29.15	2 36 17.87			
		18 2 51.22	+ 2.77	18 2 53.99	10 56 43.70	+ 4 29 52.34	15 26 36.04	2 36 17.95	17.93		
		18 28 43.92	+ 2.76	18 28 46.68	11 22 32.12	+ 4 29 56.58	15 52 28.70	2 36 17.98			
24	to C.	16 57 10.71	+ 2.15	16 57 12.86	9 47 14.76	+ 4 33 41.59	14 20 56.35	2 36 16.51			
		17 3 49.54	+ 2.15	17 3 49.54	9 53 52.33	+ 4 33 42.68	14 27 35.01	2 36 16.58	16.51		
		17 26 25.00	+ 2.16	17 26 27.16	10 16 24.33	+ 4 33 46.40	14 50 10.73	2 36 16.43			
										0.66	2 36 17.16
	C. to W.	17 12 30.06	+ 2.15	17 12 32.21	10 2 30.25	+ 4 33 44.10	14 36 14.35	2 36 17.86			
		17 19 28.81	+ 2.15	17 19 30.96	10 9 27.92	+ 4 33 45.25	14 43 13.17	2 36 17.79	17.82		

Giving each group of signals equal weight, we have, as the longitude resulting rom the work of the three nights,

$$2^{h}\ 36^{m}\ 17^{s}.24$$

As the Washington transit-instrument is $0^{s}.036$ east of the center of the dome, we have, finally, the Carlin station west of the center of the dome of the Naval Observatory,

$$2^{h}\ 36^{m}\ 17^{s}.20$$

AUSTIN, NEVADA.

Latitude, $+ 39^{\circ}\ 29'\ 21''.9$.

This station is situated in the cañon through which the road to Belmont passes. To the east of the station, a short distance above the Manhattan Mill, the land rises rapidly to Mount Prometheus; to the north there is a slope downward to the valley of the Reese River; to the south it descends a short distance to the bottom of the cañon, and then rises quite rapidly up a branch-cañon to a height of several hundred feet. Toward the west there is a descent for some distance, and then a considerable rise, to the crest of another hill.

The instrument used was a combined transit, No. 16, by Würdemann, of 26.0 inches focal length and 1.75 inches aperture. It was mounted on three pieces of redwood scantling, 4 by 4 inches, set on the hard rock at a depth of about three feet, and fastened together above the ground by cross-pieces of board.

Observations for time were made by means of a sidereal chronometer, Negus No. 1344.

For exchange of signals, a mean solar chronometer, Hutton No. 288, was used.

At the time this station was occupied there was much cloudy weather, usually clearing off about 11^h p. m. and remaining clear until the afternoon of the next day.

The observations for time at Austin were made and reduced in the same way as those made at Carlin.

AUSTIN, NEVADA, *June* 16, 1871.

Name of Star.	Clamp.	T	*b* B	*a* A	*c* C	T'	AR.	ΔT
		h. m. s.	s.	s.	s.	h. m. s.	h. m. s.	s.
η Bootis.	E.	13 48 1.08	+ 0.22	+ 0.76	− 0.36	13 48 1.70	13 48 33.64	+ 31.94
50 Cassiopeæ, L. C. .	.	13 51 47.76	− 0.25	+ 6.15	+ 1.08	13 51 54.74	13 52 26.28	31.54
α Draconis	.	14 0 26.42	+ 0.53	− 2.11	− 0.80	14 0 24.04	14 0 55.45	31.41
α Bootis.	.	9 15.28	+ 0.29	+ 0.74	− 0.36	9 15.95	9 47.80	31.85
ι Cassiopeæ, L. C. .	W.	17 50.35	− 0.12	+ 5.04	− 0.86	17 54.41	18 26.44	32.03
θ Bootis.	.	20 17 51	+ 0.28	− 0.76	+ 0.56	20 17.59	20 49.86	32.27
5 Ursæ Minoris . .	.	27 24.62	+ 0.58	− 5.20	+ 1.43	27 21.43	27 53.23	31.80
ε Bootis.	.	14 38 49.72	+ 0.13	+ 0.48	+ 0.38	14 38 50.71	14 39 22.56	+ 31.85

For $14^h\ 30^m$ local sidereal time the mean correction is $+31^s.836$.

Normal Equations.

$$0 = +\ 0.08 + 8.00\,\delta t + \ 2.47\,a' - \ 3.15\,c$$
$$0 = +\ 1.00 + 2.47\,\delta t + 22.68\,a' + \ 5.99\,c$$
$$0 = +\ 14.82 - 3.15\,\delta t + \ 5.99\,a' + 46.35\,c$$

Whence—

$$\delta t = -\,0^s.163$$
$$a' = +\,0^s.063$$
$$c = -\,0^s.339$$

Assumed azimuth constant $+\,2^s.00$; therefore the adopted azimuth constant is $= +\,2^s.063$.

AUSTIN, NEVADA, *June* 16, 1871.

Name of Star.	Clamp.	T	*b* B	*a* A	*c* C	T'	AR.	ΔT
		h. m s.	s.	s.	s.	h. m. s.	h. m. s.	s.
d Sagittarii	E.	19 9 31.40	− 0.03	+ 4.44	− 0.36	19 9 35.45	19 10 6.88	+ 31.43
δ Draconis	.	12 9.85	− 0.15	− 6.00	− 0.89	12 2.81	12 34.46	31.65
δ Aquilæ	.	18 27.26	− 0.06	+ 2.93	− 0.34	18 29.79	19 1.17	31.38
κ Aquilæ	.	29 23.80	0.00	+ 3.56	− 0.34	29 27.02	29 58.59	31.57
γ Aquilæ	.	39 35.78	+ 0.04	+ 2.39	− 0.35	39 37.86	40 9.12	31.26
α Aquilæ	.	43 57.38	+ 0.06	+ 2.54	− 0.35	43 59.63	44 30.85	31.22
ε Draconis	.	19 48 15.98	+ 0.25	− 7.22	− 0.99	19 48 8.02	19 48 39.22	+ 31.20

For $19^h\ 30^m$ local sidereal time the mean correction is $+\,31^s.387$.

Normal Equations.

$$0 = -\,0.55 + 7.00\,\delta t + 0.54\,a'$$
$$0 = +\,0.68 + 0.54\,\delta t + 5.93\,a'$$

Whence—

$$\delta t = +\,0.080$$
$$a' = -\,0.122$$

Assumed azimuth constant $+\,5^s.00$; therefore the adopted azimuth constant is $4^s.878$.

Hence the correction to sidereal chronometer Negus No. 1344 for $17^h\ 0^m$ local sidereal time is $+31^s.612$, and its rate is $-\,0^s.042$.

For the exchange of signals, the mean solar chronometer Hutton No. 288 was employed.

Some mistake was made in comparing Hutton No. 288 with Negus No. 1344 before the exchange of signals, and the rate of Hutton No. 288 was derived from the following comparisons:

Date.	Negus No. 1344.	Hutton No. 288.
	h. m. s.	h. m. s.
June 16.5	18 45 48.0	12 45 8.75
17.0	6 44 37.0	0 41 59.5

By means of the correction and rate of Negus No. 1344, the following correction and rate for Hutton No. 288 are deduced:

Date.	Time by Hutton.	Correction to Local Sidereal Time.	Hourly Rate.
1871.	h. m. s.	h. m. s.	s.
June 16.5	12 45 8.75	+ 6 1 10.79	+ 9.8561

This correction and rate is used for Hutton No. 288, at the time of exchange of signals.

Date.	Signals sent from—	Time of Mean of Signals by Washington Clock.	Correction of Washington Clock.	Local Sidereal Time of Mean of Signals.	Time of Mean of Signals by Austin Chronometer.	Correction of Austin Chronometer.	Local Sidereal Time of Mean of Signals.	Differences of Longitude.	Means.	Wave and Armature Time.	Final differ'nce of Longitude.
1871.		h. m. s.	s.	h. m. s.	h. m. s.	h. m. s.	h. m. s.	h. m. s.	s.	s.	h. m. s.
June 16	W. to A.	20 16 0.00	− 2.27	20 15 57.73	11 34 56.16	+ 6 0 59.26	17 35 55.42	2 40 2.31	2.32		
		20 38 15.40	− 2.28	20 38 13.12	11 57 7.90	+ 6 1 2.90	17 58 10.80	2 40 2.32		0.61	2 40 2.93
	A. to W.	20 25 19.37	− 2.27	20 25 17.10	11 44 12.74	+ 6 1 0.78	17 45 13.52	2 40 3.58			
		20 49 0.41	− 2.28	20 48 58.13	12 7 50.00	+ 6 1 4.65	18 8 54.65	2 40 3.48	3.54		
		20 58 57.63	− 2.28	20 58 55.35	12 17 45.50	+ 6 1 6.29	18 18 51.79	2 40 3.56			

The exchange of signals on June 16 gives, therefore, a difference of longitude of—

$$2^h\ 40^m\ 2^s.93$$

Applying the correction, $-0^s.036$, for the position of the transit-instrument at Washington, we have the observing-station at Austin, Nevada, west of the center of the dome of the Naval Observatory,

$$2^h\ 40^m\ 2^s.89$$

No opportunity was afforded me to obtain any observations to determine the value of the personal equation between Mr. Austin and myself, and I have, consequently, been delayed nearly two years in the preparation of this report.

Much of the success in exchanging signals was due to the careful arrangement of the temporary system of wires and connections in the Observatory by Mr. W. F. Gardner, and to the kindness and peculiar skill of Mr. M. M. Marean, who had charge of the transmission and reception of messages.

Very respectfully, your obedient servant,

J. R. EASTMAN,

Professor of Mathematics, United States Navy.

Rear-Admiral C. H. DAVIS, U. S. N.,

Superintendent United States Naval Observatory.

www.ingramcontent.com/pod-product-compliance
Lightning Source LLC
LaVergne TN
LVHW020632110826
845149LV00004B/1150

* 9 7 8 1 4 1 8 1 8 6 6 6 1 *